LOSERS, USERS & PARASITES:

A Host's Guide to Ridding Your Life

of Unwanted People

LOSERS, USERS & PARASITES:

A Host's Guide to Ridding Your Life
of Unwanted People

by

Lance Q. Zedric

Pathfinder Publishing
Ventura, California

LOSERS, USERS & PARASITES

Published by:
Pathfinder Publishing of California
458 Dorothy Avenue
Ventura, CA 93003
(805) 642-9278

Library of Congress Cataloging-in-Publication Data

Zedric, Lance Q., 1961-
  Losers, users & parasites : a host's guide to ridding your life of unwanted people / by Lance Q. Zedric.
      p.   cm.
  Includes index.
  ISBN 0-934793-61-1
  1. Interpersonal conflict. 2. Manipulative behavior.
  3. Interpersonal relations. 4. Conflict management. I. Title.
  BF637.I48Z33 1996
  158'.2—dc20   96-22252
                                                        CIP

DEDICATION

To my grandmother, "Doom,"—

With eternal love.

Lance

ACKNOWLEDGMENTS

I wish to thank the countless people across the country who shared their sometimes painful, often funny, and always sincere accounts which constitute the body of this book. In interviewing them for the project, they were open, honest, and forthcoming. In many cases, all I had to do was strike up a conversation and tell them the title of the book, and they ran with it. Most chuckled and began telling me about the people who had used them. They made it easy.

My family, friends, co-workers, and a few bartenders, also deserve special recognition. Thanks to Mark Skiles, Tom Meiron, Al Pherigo, Dave Wright, and Jack Culp for their unwavering belief in the absolute fallibility of human nature; to Mike Rock and Debbie R., for providing constant inspiration: to Garvin Chadwell for his unmatched humor and unique perspective on life: to Bob Stack for his support and guidance, and to my Mother, Peggy, for her valuable input and understanding, eclectic gene pool, and the best fried chicken on earth, but most of all for her love.

Lastly, thanks to Eugene and Eugenie Wheeler, and to the staff of Pathfinder Publishing for being supportive and helpful.

IT WAS FUN!

CONTENTS

INTRODUCTION

We are all users. It's that simple. From the moment we realize as children that throwing a screaming fit in the checkout isle of a grocery store will get us the candy bar we want, or that preparing a romantic dinner and treating our mate to an evening of passion is the most effective "can I have this or that" tool in the game, we learn to use.

As normal adults we understand that we give and take to varying degrees in every relationship, and we accept it as a fact of life. If we didn't, buses wouldn't run, men wouldn't buy diamond rings, women wouldn't get pregnant, and nothing would ever get accomplished!

But unfortunately, some people get used too often while others use too much. The LOSERS, USERS and PARASITES of life, or LUPs for short, are the people who always take, never give back, keep coming back, and are damn near impossible to get rid of. The HOSTS, on the other hand, are those people who attract and take care of the LUPs, whether they want to or not. This book is about both.

If you are tired of hosting "needy" people who drain your time, energy, money, and anything else of value, this book may be of some help. If you are tired of being a "LUP magnet" who stumbles through life wearing a "I'M A HOST—USE ME!" sign on your forehead, and you are truly prepared and determined to exterminate the bloodsuckers in your life, please read on.

1

THE HOST

Parasitism: Great fleas have little fleas upon their backs to bite 'em,
And little fleas have lesser fleas, and so ad infinitum.
Augustus De Morgan

The world is full of losers, users and parasites (LUPs). Although they appear in many forms; family, friends, lovers, co-workers, men, women, children, etc., they all have one thing in common. Every LUP needs a living, breathing host to survive. Without one they will die.

Before identifying the several types of LUPs, it is important to first identify the characteristics of the host. The first step in ridding yourself of pesky parasites is understanding what it is about YOU that ATTRACTS them.

To determine if you're a potential host, take the following Host Test and answer each question truthfully:

1. Do you have a lot of money?
2. Do you have trouble saying "no"?
3. Are your feelings easily hurt?
4. Are you too generous?
5. Do you need to be liked?
6. Are you gullible?
7. Do you hate being alone?
8. Do you NEED to be NEEDED?
9. Are you too nice?
10. Do people make you feel guilty?

If you answered "yes" to any of these questions, chances are you would make an excellent host for the swarming hoards of LUPs just waiting to latch on to a free lunch. Naturally, anyone with lots of money is a prime target. People are always trying to get into your pocket and help share your good fortune. But having money doesn't necessarily mean that you would make a good host, only a good target. If you answered "yes" to any one of questions 2-10, watch out! It's a pretty safe bet that you would make a fine host.

Let's take a brief look at each question and ask yourself if they apply to you.

NUMBER 2: If you answered "yes," be careful. Your inability to say "no" is paramount to wearing a bright red bullseye on your shirt. LUPs can see it a mile away. They will descend upon you like vultures on roadkill and pick your bones dry. You must learn to say NO! Contrary to what you may think, it's easier to say no to a large LUP request, such as "Can I borrow $10,000," than it is to refuse to baby-sit your sister's kids on a Saturday night. So, take the opposite approach and begin conditioning yourself to say "NO" to larger requests. As you begin to feel more comfortable turning people down, it will become second nature. Who knows, you might even like it!

NUMBER 3: Are your feelings easily hurt? Over-sensitivity, lack of self-esteem, and low self-confidence, are gold-plated, engraved invitations to a LUP feast—of course, at your expense. Thin-skinned people are always prime targets. LUPs know exactly which emotional buttons to push to get what they want. "If you really cared you'd help me out," or "I thought if there was anyone I could count on it would be you, but ..." Sound familiar?

Of course, it's easy for someone else to tell you to be less sensitive or to be more confident. But it's not that simple. Everyone lacks self-esteem at some point in their life and it's often hard to regain it once it's lost. But if you want to thicken your skin to LUP attacks, recognize that your feelings are a soft spot and try not to wear them on your sleeve.

NUMBER 4: Are you too generous? Ouch! This one hurts! If you want to see where excessive generosity will land you, run an advertisement in your local newspaper and announce that you will be giving $5 bills away to the first 10,000 callers. Major thoroughfares will be spilling over with LUPs from all corners of the earth and you will never again have time to sleep, eat, make love, or do anything for yourself again. You will be too busy giving away everything you own. If you feel that you are too generous, stop and ask yourself why? What does it do for you? Does it give you a warm and fuzzy feeling all over your body? Does it pay your rent or fulfill some gaping void in your life? Get real! Figure out what you "really" get out of giving and ask yourself if it's "really" worth the price.

NUMBER 5: Do you need everyone to like you? If you answered "yes" to this one, you're in big trouble. What better way to win friends than to give them something valuable. Whether its money, time, blood, a kidney, whatever, friends can be bought (temporarily), especially LUPs. For example, in

1969, I had the dubious honor of being the new, fat, redheaded kid in school. I was desperate for "friends" and I promptly decided to go shopping for some with my father's valuable and very old silver dollar collection. I doled them out freely to all the kids on the school bus. Behold! I had friends coming out of the woodwork! EVERYONE LIKED ME! Except my dad. But once the silver dollars were gone so were my friends. The next day, all I had to show for it was a red butt. Accept the fact that not everyone will like you. Some people will dislike you for no reason and others will dislike you for their own reasons, neither of which you should worry about. Like yourself. It's cheaper and a lot less hassle.

NUMBER 6: Are you gullible? For many people, this is a tough question to answer. Some people are gullible when it comes to money, others with the opposite sex, some with both. Do you fall into the category with those who buy every get rich quick scheme that comes down the pike? Do you believe everything you read in tabloids or everything the government tells you? If you do, you will believe the polished and cunning LUP. Open your eyes.

Shakespeare once wrote that "A rose is a rose is a rose, by any other name smells as sweet." But when it comes to believing a LUP sob-story, there's another old saying that fits quite nicely: "If it looks like shit, smells like shit, and tastes like shit; chances are it's shit! Be skeptical.

NUMBER 7: Do you hate being alone? If you answered "yes" to this question, it doesn't necessarily mean that you would make a good host, but it does imply that you have the potential to be one. A lot of people dislike being alone and enjoy the constant presence of others. But be careful. A LUP knows this and is often quick to become a full-time companion; one who will gladly trade their time and companionship for your money, a place to stay, favors, and anything of value. Think of them as a companion for sale.

NUMBER 8: Do you need to be needed? Everyone likes to be needed to a degree. But if you NEED to be needed, you might as well sign your car and bank account over right now. Because there are plenty of LUPs who NEED you to NEED them. By answering "yes," you are also close to treading in your own parasitic waters. In other words, you will unknowingly seek out a LUP to fulfill your own needs. A mutual co-existence, but one that will cost you far more than it will the LUP.

Again, a little self-examination will go a long way toward realizing and dealing with your neediness. What is it that you need by being needed? Do you feel more "worthy?" Do you feel more loved? If this particular psychological monkey is climbing on your back, shake him off fast or the LUPs will soon have you in the soup line NEEDING a handout!

NUMBER 9: Are you too nice? First of all, let's define what it is to be nice. If giving to every beggar, bum, freeloader, and bloodsucker that comes along is being too nice; then yes, you are too nice. But if it's giving to bonified charities, school programs, needy children, then no. You ARE nice. Don't confuse nice with gullible. There are a lot of nice sensible, strong, shrewd, and charitable people in the world. The key is not being too nice and not wanting or being able to hurt someone's feelings when they are clearly trying to use or take advantage of you.

NUMBER 10: Do people make you feel guilty. This question is sickening to write about, but it's one of the most important ones in the Host Test. Guilt is a strong motivater. It compels us to do things that we wouldn't ordinarily do. Internal guilt, such as feeling remorse for knowingly accepting overpayment at the grocery store without mentioning it, or sleeping with your best friend's husband while she's caring for her sick mother, can be helpful and make us do the right thing because it's the right thing to do.

But guilt trips laid on by others can be costly, especially when they cause us to do something that we KNOW isn't right or that will cost us in the long run. Whenever someone tries to make you feel guilty, ask yourself what that person has to gain by making you feel that way, then ask yourself what you have to lose. Is it self-righteousness, envy, lust, greed, sloth, avarice, or a host of other SINS, or is it simply that they know you'll give them what they want if you're made to feel guilty enough? Remember, guilt trains run every day, all day. If you want to get anywhere in life, this is one conveyance you don't need to ride!

THE BIG SET UP

If after taking the Host Test you realize that you are a potential host, the second step in avoiding LUPs is to understand HOW you set YOURSELF up for the big bite. More often than not we get LUPPED because we ask for it, whether we realize it or not. Although a person may have the personality traits of a host, they can decrease their chances of getting used by steering clear of LUP breeding grounds.

As with so many things in life, being at the right place at the right time, or in this case, being at the wrong place at the wrong time, is often the key to success or failure. One doesn't look for a virgin in a delivery room, nor does one hunt bees in the nude, while dipped in honey expecting not to get stung. It isn't any different when it comes to hosting a LUP gala. One of the best defenses is simply to not send out invitations.

When you're in the company of known LUPs there are a few basic and general principles (specific strategies will come later in the book) you should adhere to. Otherwise, you will set yourself up. Remember, these principles do not necessarily apply to those you trust, only to LUPs:

1. NEVER talk about or show how much money you have. It's better to cry poor than to become poor. A person who goes around spouting off about how much money they have, or "flash-

ing the cash" to everyone, is a marked person. But if a LUP thinks you're as broke as he/she is, they'll move on.

2. NEVER offer a favor. Always suggest an exchange or trade off for something instead. But insure that you get what you want first, or you will get stiffed. LUPs would much rather receive than give, and if everything has a price, it won't be long before they're gone.

3. NEVER put your total faith in the goodness of human nature. Like the old proverb states; Trust but VERIFY.

All this caution and distrust may seem excessive, but we live in a real world. We don't live alone on a mountain top in Tibet contemplating the greater existence of mankind, or sit in a rose garden all day eating ambrosia and nectar basking in our endless good fortune. The fact is, we only have so much energy, so much money, and so much time on earth. We can't click our heels together three times and wake up in Kansas, and expect everyone to do what is right by us. We have to take control of our own lives. If we don't, someone else will take control for us.

"Everything looks so good! You two are the best hosts."

2

THE MOSQUITO

MOSQUITOES: Flying insects with a damnably poisonous bite, which every one except hotel managers has seen, heard, or suffered from.

Edward Verrall Lucas

From the Neanderthal caveman to the modern day astronaut, mosquitoes have pissed off and irritated more people than any creature on earth. Therefore, the first and most prevalent type of LUP is aptly named the mosquito, but is more commonly known as the "mooch." For the purpose of this chapter, the mooch is defined as the LUP that borrows and uses "things."

We all know at least one person who delights in begging and borrowing anything and everything from us and never pays back. It is their nature. Like mosquitoes, "mooches" land on our most vulnerable spot, insert their stingers, and suck out as much blood as possible. Sometimes they strike silently, without warning, and it isn't until we feel the welt that we realize we've been stung. Other times they're as loud as a main street parade and we can see and hear them coming a mile away. Although mosquito bites, like paper cuts, are rarely fatal, they are among life's most painful annoyances.

Family members, friends, or both, are often the worst mosquitoes of all. Surprisingly, most are employed and can afford to buy their own food, drinks, books, makeup, cigarettes, clothes, and all the little things in life. But why should they spend their money on such trivial items when there are so many available hosts out there?

Before looking at some specific examples of mosquito LUPs and how to protect ourselves against them, it is important to distinguish between those people who innocently need and borrow from us, as opposed to those who are sharpening their stingers. **Be careful not to confuse sincere give-and-take friendship with parasitic feeding.** But, on the other hand, if the blood is too sweet, we can turn even our most trusted and loyal friends and family members into mosquitoes without even realizing it.

If you have read this far and are nodding your head in agreement, chances are you've been stung real good and want to learn more about the mosquito LUP and how it operates. Unfortunately, it is impossible to expose every breed buzzing around out there. But listed below are examples of the most common types. Take note of how many times you've been stung and get your repellent ready!

The Bucks LUP

The next best thing to throwing money away, or setting it on fire, is to own your own bucks LUP. The term not only refers to those LUPs who constantly borrow money, but also those whose behavior costs money. Since this chapter deals with mosquito-type behavior, it will focus only on those LUPs who "nickel and dime" a person to death, not the big-money users. Those scurrilous parasites will be addressed in later chapters.

How many times have you heard "I'm running a little short, can I borrow a couple bucks?" or "I didn't have a chance to go to the bank, can you spot me five until next time?" Other favorites are "How much cash you got on you? Loan me some and I'll write you a check when we get back to YOUR place," or "Do you have 75 cents on you? I don't want to break a dollar!" Suddenly, you're on the spot and feeling like a rape victim. You know you've been violated and you didn't like it one bit!

Every host has a "friend" who loves to go out for a night on the town and never brings enough money. After they offer to buy the first drink you're excited. You believe that they finally brought enough money and that instead of waking up in the morning with no money and a headache, you will only have a headache. But your hopes are soon dashed.

After they've bought one beer you're stuck with picking up the tab for the rest of evening. To your horror, your friend switches from beer and starts drinking those exotic, expensive concoctions with tiny umbrellas in them!

But it's not only friends who bite you in bars. People who knew you in high school fifteen years ago, and didn't give a damn about you then, are suddenly your friends again. And to your chagrin, they need a couple of bucks to buy groceries and feed the kids. They swear on their mother's grave and on their sacred honor that they'll pay you back. Violin music begins to play in your head. The poor LUP is almost in tears. Your defenses weaken. You think "What's a few dollars?" Moments later, you spot the LUP sitting happily in front of a "win every time" poker machine drinking a beer, gambling away your money, and smoking your last cigarette! BUZZZZZ!

Restaurants are also great LUP feeding grounds. You've just finished a wonderfully expensive meal with your "friend" and the waitress shows up at your table with the check and says "Will this be together or on separate checks?" Your friend invites the waitress to "put them on one ticket," and then slyly throws out a couple bucks and says "I've got the tip."

Another favorite is the old "restroom" trick. As you walk to the cash register to pay the bill, your friend disappears into the restroom. What seems like an hour later, which is ample time to pay the bill and to urinate, your friend returns and promises that the next time dinner will be "on him/her." A third LUP tactic is to develop a severe case of alligator arms. That is, when it comes to paying the bill their arms grow too short to reach to the bottom of their pockets and they are unable to find their portion of the bill.

Along those same lines, LUPs are notorious for pretending to fumble through their wallets and purses in search of money while their friends pay the bill. Occasionally, you will run into the user friend who only has a $100.00 bill to pay for a couple of hot dogs and drinks at a football game. You pay because the vendor hasn't change for the century note. Surprise! After the second trick, send him a bill.

Solution

One way of avoiding getting stung is asking your friend how much money they have before going out. This way your friend knows that they won't be able to suck off of you all night and that they will have to foot their fair share of the bill. If they don't have any or much money on them, kindly offer to drive them to the Automatic Teller Machine to get some. If you really want to send a clear message that you won't be used as a human ATM, ask them if YOU can borrow some money and pay them back later! Remember, a parasite can't live off another parasite for very long.

The Clothes LUP

"That outfit is so cute! Can I wear it?" In other words, I'm too tight to buy it and hopefully you'll forget that I have it!" This recurring plea has haunted more people than the Ghost of Christmas Past. Family members are notorious for this, especially women. Whether its dresses, shoes, jewelry, purses, or cosmetics, female LUPs love to borrow, covet, and keep clothing and personal accessories. It doesn't matter to the clothes LUP if the blouse is the wrong size or that the shoes are a little big, all that matters is that they are using someone else's property and that it doesn't cost them a dime.

Solutions

It's never easy refusing a friend or a family member, but if you miraculously find that you have more empty hangers than ever before, something has to be done. When a simple "no" is out of the question or when it won't phase the threadbare LUP, it's time to take a more passive (aggressive) approach. Short of sabotaging every dress with itching powder, most women say that the best LUP deterrent is role reversal.

"My sister used to call and ask if I wanted to go shopping or go out to a night club," said one woman. "Whenever she came over to pick me up she wouldn't be wearing any makeup. She would always help herself to mine and then go through my closet looking for an outfit. I'd let her 'borrow' my clothes, but I'd never get them back. After a half-dozen outfits and several compacts I turned the tables and began going to her house and doing the same thing to her. She stopped 'borrowing' after that!"

The Mosquito: "I'm running low on cash—better look for a place to fill up!"

The Tool LUP

Men, on the other hand, are infamous tool borrowers. Again, family members and friends are often the worst culprits. Every man who has ever owned a tool has heard "I just need to borrow a couple of wrenches. I'll have them back to you as soon as I'm finished," or "I'll put them back Dad, I swear." Yeah, the check's in the mail, too. It's no wonder that every garage in the free world has posted a sign reading "We don't loan tools, so don't ask!" If they did they would be out of business in two weeks.

Self-professed shade-tree mechanics and Bob Villa wannabees quickly turn into full-fledged LUPs when they realize how expensive tools are, especially when they have to reach into their own pockets to pay for them. Normally, the first few times that a tool LUP borrows a tool they promptly return it unbroken, clean, and fully intact. But beware. He's setting his prey up for the big sting. After he's gained the lender's confidence, he borrows more often and takes longer to return the tool. Suddenly, dad's or brother's tools become even more attractive and less returnable. With tool LUPs on the prowl, a full 64-piece socket set mysteriously diminishes to an effete 8-piece starter kit. A shiny new shovel is returned to its owner with a cracked handle and two pounds of mud on it, or a $20 wrench becomes a homing device for a lawnmower blade.

After years of lending his tools to four well-meaning but highly-forgetful sons, my grandfather devised his own system of warding off tool LUPs and insuring that his tools always found their way home. Upon getting any new tool he would immediately retreat to the safety of his heavily secured garage and paint the wooden handle of every last tool bright red and the business end glossy black. This way there was no mistaking who owned the tool, partly because no one else would go to all the effort of painting them! Afterwards, he would hang the tool on a pegboard and paint an outline around it so he could tell if it was missing. Naturally, the garage door was secured with a padlock that Harry Houdini couldn't pick. But despite his security measures, he still

24

fell prey to his innovative sons who each managed to come up with a key. Today, his pegboard is nearly empty.

Solutions

As the preceding story illustrates no man is safe from a tool LUP, but there are a few measures you can take to insure that your pegboard is not left bare.

The simplest and most effective way to derail a tool LUP is to never lend the first tool. But as is often the case, it's hard to turn down family and friends. So, we live with it. If you've been victimized by a tool LUP you understand how frustrating it is to reach for the power saw only to remember that you loaned it out six months ago and that the man has since moved. One sure way of getting tools back is to charge a cash deposit, preferably one that is more than the cost of the tool. Make the person sign their name to a receipt stating that the tool will be returned within a specified period of time and in the same or better condition than when it was borrowed. A $10 deposit for a screwdriver will work wonders. A true blue LUP will either refuse and fly off to another host, or guard the safety of the screwdriver with their life. It's as simple as that.

The Food LUP

There is such a thing as a free lunch, especially when family and friends are involved. Every human being is guilty of being a food LUP at one time or the other. We all know what time our parents, grandparents, family, neighbors, and friends sit down to have a meal, and in turn, they know what time we eat. Isn't it amazing that often the only time we visit them, or are visited by them, is at mealtime. Sadly, a free lunch is often the only bait which lures family and friends over. Of course, breaking bread with friends and loved ones has been a ritual for thousands of years and continues to bond people together. But when mealtime becomes the **only** time we see those people or that they see us, it begins to border on parasitic behavior. Worse yet, is when the person comes over right after a 40-day fast and gorges themselves!

But it isn't just at mealtime that the food LUP strikes. Some LUPs enter your home and make a beeline for the refrigerator. After they've foraged through the ice box and devoured the leftovers that were going to be your next meal, they often "have to run." This type of LUP is also a frequent food borrower and has no shame in borrowing a cup of this and a cup of that until they can "get to the store."

The coffee LUP fits nicely into this category of hungry mosquitoes, too. To them the "best part of waking up is someone else's coffee in their cup!" The coffee LUP, however, is more subtle and sometimes has a hidden agenda. The coffee is only a tool to get in the door and soften the skin. An apparently innocent visit to just chat over a cup of Joe can turn into a full-fledged setup for something bigger. "Oh, by the way as long as I'm here, can I borrow..." BZZZZZ!

Businesses are very vulnerable to the coffee LUP. Those that have a pot of free coffee brewing are prime targets for the swarms of bean pounders. Take note of how little business the coffee LUPs do at your establishment. They arrive early in the morning when the coffee is fresh and drink half a pot, but they never stop by to patronize the business or even offer to pitch in for the coffee.

Solutions

There is no easy solution to deter the food and coffee LUP, but there are few things you can do to fend him off for a while without changing your mealtime, keeping an empty refrigerator, and giving up coffee. First, take a mental note of when the LUP usually visits. At those certain times prepare a meal that you like but one that he/she doesn't. A steady ration of liver and onions and blood pudding will deter most people from coming over for a meal. Second, put them to work. Every time the LUP comes over have a few "chores" that they can help you with, such as moving heavy furniture or cleaning the bathroom. Naturally, have them help before they sit down to eat. They will quickly learn that a meal will cost them something, and it's up them to decide what they're willing to pay. Either way, it may cost you a meal but you get some work done. Afterwards, ask them to help clean off the table or help wash the dishes. The double whammie should seal the deal. If that doesn't work, next time prepare their plate for them and add a lot of hot sauce! A big heartburn should send your message.

Dealing with the coffee LUP is much easier. Again, it's important to know when the LUP normally stops by so you can plan a strategy. Tell them you're out of coffee and ask them to go to the local convenience store and buy a pound of coffee—this tactic will soon curb their thirst for your coffee. Another method is to buy the cheapest, rudest Turkish coffee you can find and serve it only when they come over. A mouthful of bitter coffee grounds will usually halt most American's excessive coffee drinking. At the workplace, simply move the coffee pot behind the counter or away from where the LUP can reach it. Asking them to make a fresh pot every time they come in also seems to dent their appetite for your coffee. If that doesn't work consider opening a cafe.

Underlying solutions to the dilemma of being caught in a parasite's web is the will and skill to say NO. Experts in assertive training stress that you have to feel that you have the right to say NO before you can say it effectively. So, whether it's a tool, your car, book, time, space, or money, begin with telling yourself that you have the right to have and to hold these things in your own way. You have a right to refuse to share them, or to share them only on your own terms.

The Auto LUP

"Can I borrow your car to run to the grocery store? I'll just be gone a few minutes." AAAAAAAARRRGGGG! Foul! Foul! Nothing is more sacred or more cherished by Americans than their automobile. It symbolizes their independence and reflects their individuality more than any single thing in their lives, and the greatest imposition of all is when an auto LUP asks to borrow their car. It is not only an inconvenience but it takes away their freedom to come and go as they wish. Owners have enough difficulty making their car payments, paying outrageous insurance rates, and filling their gas tanks for their own use without shouldering the burden of buying fuel for auto LUPs. Of course, most everyone has gladly loaned their automobile to a friend or family member for an emergency or use at one time or another, but constant borrowing is intolerable.

A five-minute run to the grocery store often turns into an out-of-town or several hour trip, one which costs the lender a tank of gasoline, wear-and-tear on the automobile, and occasionally a fender bender or parking ticket. How many times have you loaned your car out only to have it returned with food wrappers or soda cans laying on the floorboard of the passenger side? How many times have you discovered cigarette burns on the seat, chipped paint on the door, or a broken window handle after loaning your car to an unappreciative and irresponsible auto LUP?

Having an auto LUP in the family or having one as a friend can be very expensive. When an auto LUP burns a full tank of gasoline and fails to refill it, it costs you double. You've not only lost the money that it took to fill your tank the first time, but the cost of refilling it. Unfortunately, paying for a tank of gasoline is often the most inexpensive result. "I let my best friend use my truck one time," said a friend from Illinois. "He not only ran my tank dry, he also bent my grill and dented in my door. That was the last time I ever let him use my truck!"

Solution

One solution to steer auto LUPs away from using your automobile is to use them as your own taxi driver and to run errands for you. Whenever they honk their borrowing horn send them on a useful trip for you. As soon as they ask to borrow your car politely say "Sure, but there are a few things I need you to do while you're out. Mail these letters for me at the post office, stop by the grocery store (make sure it's the busiest one in town), buy a gallon of milk, have the car washed, pick up Johnny and Susie from school, and put gas in my car." Of course, the "errands" can be whatever you want them to be, and that the LUP has to spend a lot of THEIR time and energy on YOU. The strategy works even better if your gas tank is nearly on "E." That way the LUP has to spend their money to put gas in YOUR tank! Even if the LUPs borrowing persists, you have a "go-fer" at your disposal. If they complain that they don't have time to help you out, simply say "I can't let you borrow my car. As you know, I have errands to run!" That puts you in a win/win situation. You either loan your automobile and get your errands taken care of or they refuse and you don't have to loan your car. After a few all-day errand runs most auto LUPs will speed away from you as fast as they can.

The Book LUP

To the avid reader nothing is more injurious than loaning a book to someone and never getting it back. Most readers normally delight in passing on a good story to a friend or family member so they can enjoy the same intellectual and emotional fulfillment. But that delight quickly sours when a signed first edition never finds its way back home and you're left feeling like the book-of-the-month-club. Anyone who has ever owned a collection of books has likely experienced this trauma and felt the jagged teeth of the Book LUP. This covetous creature is guilty of no less than literary larceny and should be treated accordingly.

"I prefer to buy hardback books," lamented Peggy, "and they get quite expensive. It seemed like every time I bought a bestseller my best friend would ask to borrow it so she wouldn't have to buy a copy for herself. After a month or so I would politely ask my friend if she had finished reading the book. I was really trying to tell her that I wanted my book back, but she kept putting me off by saying that she hadn't had time to read it yet. I made a point to visit her one afternoon and as I was snooping through her books I discovered that she had several of my books and many of the pages were dog-eared and marked on. She lied to me and had no intention of returning them."

I once had a very old set of Edward Gibbon's The History of the Decline and Fall of the Roman Empire, *" added Dan, a former graduate student. A friend asked to borrow one of the volumes to research a term paper for a history final. Against my better judgment, I loaned it to him. I never saw him or the book again. He graduated and returned to Chicago and now my set is incomplete and virtually worthless. I should have known better.*

Solutions

If you have been victimized by a Book LUP, but still insist on operating your own public library, there are some steps you can take to minimize the risk of continually restocking your shelves. First, invest in personalized bookplates or a seal (like those used by notaries) with your name on it. Attach a bookplate or affix a seal on the inside cover of each book, or on a blank page inside the book. Next, before lending the book, write the bibliographical information, such as the name of the book, publication date, and author, on an index card, also include the replacement price of the book. Have the borrower write their name, address, and phone number, along with the date they received the book, on the card. Then have them sign it. This may not guarantee the return of a book, but it increases the odds. Not only does the potential LUP know that they are responsible for it, THEY know that YOU know that THEY know they are responsible for it.

If this doesn't work and you're still gullible enough to loan books, make the LUP read the book at your house!

The Tobacco LUP

Every smoker knows one. The tobacco LUP is simply too tight, too lazy, or too broke to buy their own cigarettes. How many times have you pulled out a smoke and just barely got it to your mouth before you heard a familiar buzz over your shoulder? "Can I borrow a cigarette? Do you have an extra smoke?" After a while it becomes maddening! It's usually a friend who only smokes when you smoke and feels no guilt in inhaling away your hard-earned money. What they are really saying is "why should I smoke my cigarettes when you are stupid enough to keep giving yours away?" As if a LUP hovering over you isn't bad enough, many have the gall to ask for a light! Five obligatory minutes later, after hanging around to smoke YOUR cigarette with YOU, the LUP casually strolls away in search of the next human cigarette machine. Oddly, tobacco LUPs use the same excuse; "I just smoked my last one."

Solutions

There are several ways to fend off the cigarette mosquito. The best method is to charge for every cigarette. At .25 cents a cigarette, it won't take the LUP long to realize that they are paying $5 a pack to smoke your cigarettes. Another way is offering to sell them an entire pack, of course at an inflated price. If that doesn't work, invest in a package of exploding cigarette loads. After having a few cigarettes blow up their face and being the butt of your nauseating laughter, most LUPs will be reluctant to "borrow" a cigarette. But for the LUP who persists in mooching off you, a well-placed horse or human hair inserted inside a cigarette might do the trick. The smell and taste of burning hair will discourage even the most hard-core tobacco LUP. If none of these strategies works for you, just say no.

HELPFULL SKILL FOR SAYING NO!

Another handy skill when you want to say NO, but don't want to antagonize the parasite/user unnecessarily is the so-called "Two Step NO."

By acknowledging that they have a right to ASK (which they do), and then saying NO, the theory is that you come across as rejecting the request only, not the person asking. For example, "I can see that you really need the car, but NO, I don't lend it out."

Or "you do look good in my jacket, and I'm sure you could use it, but I don't choose to give it away." Try that on for size, especially if you need to refuse to do something for someone that you really want to stay friends with.

CONCLUSION

No one can go through life without being stung by a mosquito LUP. It happens to everyone, regardless of whether they are a corporate CEO, a middle class factory worker, or a ditchdigger. As long as we have contact with people we will either allow ourselves to be taken advantage of or be slyly duped by the mosquito LUP. The key to minimizing the number of stings is to douse ourselves with emotional repellent. Learn not to fall for every sob story that comes down the pike, and weed out the con-artists. Recognize that you are not the savior of the human race and that it's not solely your responsibility to feed, clothe, and support every down-on-their luck hobo or friend or family member. If you continue to subsidize and reward parasitic behavior you will be rewarded with the same. Remember, there are only as many LUPs as there are victims/hosts. Grow thick skin.

TO DO LIST

1. Identify the Mosquito LUPs in your life by writing their names down on a sheet of paper. Under each name list their Mosquito type behavior and where and when it usually occurs.
2. Look for commonalities.
3. Monitor the suspected LUPs by keeping a journal. Write down every parasitic behavior for one month. At the end of the month tally up the monetary total. Can you afford to continue as a host? Do you want to?
4. Develop a strategy for curbing or eliminating the LUP behavior.
5. Avoid situations and places where you are most often stung.
6. Avoid the people who use you. Cultivate new and positive friendships.
7. After the second month, re-examine your journal and note the monetary total and how it has changed.
8. Begin charging a fee for your "things."
9. Reward yourself each time a LUP or their behavior is eliminated from your life.

Losers, Users & Parasites

3

TICKS

TICKS: Any of numerous bloodsucking parasitic, louselike arachnids.

Now that you have toughened your skin and alerted your antennae to mosquito attacks, are you ready to take on a more insidious parasite? That's right. It gets worse. The Tick LUP is the next enemy in a long line of hard-to-kill parasites. While the Mosquito LUP targets possessions or things, such as those described in Chapter Two, the tick zeroes in on your time. Just remember "Ticks take time," which often costs you more in the long run. The nature of the tick is to attach itself to you and slowly drain your blood, or in this case your time and energy. Like the tick itself, Tick LUPs are seasonal and are only a threat at certain times. Unlike the mosquito, which you sometimes hear coming, the tick is always silent and it's not until you begin feeling him that you're even aware that he's attached. Remember, the tick will only feed until he's full and then drop off... but he will be back.

The Love-Lorn LUP

The telephone rings and it's your long-lost "best friend" and she's just been jilted for the nineteenth time of her life. You cringe and prepare yourself for the emotional onslaught that you know will follow. You're painfully aware that the **only** time you ever hear from this person is when **their** love life is on the rocks.

Normally, in a give-and-take relationship you would gladly act as a sounding board for your heartbroken friend, but when this person calls you know that you're about to be used. These so-called "Foul weather friends" or "Love-Lorn LUPs" are among life's most ravenous parasites. They normally attach themselves by telephone and devour your time and energy. When their love life returns to normal you don't hear from them again until the next *crisis amore*.

After spending hours on the phone with them over the course of two weeks it's you who needs marital counseling and is ready to be committed to a mental institution to regain your senses and physical strength. Even more maddening is when the time comes that you need someone to talk to about your troubled romance, that person is harder to find than Amelia Earhart!

"I had one lovesick friend who only came around when he was having trouble with his girlfriend," said a friend. "He interfered with every facet of my life. He called me late at night, early in the morning, and at work. He talked for hours and said the same thing over and over again. When I tried to give him suggestions he just kept talking. All I did was listen and it got old fast. He often stopped by my place and asked if I wanted to go out drinking and meet some women. We'd go to some expensive club and all he did was talk about was

Ticks

his damn girlfriend! He wasted my time and it got to the point where I didn't want to answer the phone or the doorbell!"

Solutions

It is very hard to turn away (or get away from) a Love-Lorn LUP once they've latched onto a breathing, but not necessarily willing host. Without investing in "caller ID" to screen your telephone calls, hiding your vehicle in the back yard, or not answering the doorbell, the best way to detach a Love-Lorn LUP is become very unsympathetic. This strategy also works well on, "Woe Is Me, Crying Shoulder, Hypochondriac, and Whiner LUPs." Unlike excuses, which run out after a while, a lack of sympathy will "vinegarize" your blood and make it less appetizing to the Love-Lorn LUP. Instead of playing Ann Landers or Dr. Ruth, act like a rude porter who refuses to handle the LUP's romantic baggage. Take the opposite view on everything. Siding with their "deposed" mate on every issue, whether you do or not, will quickly sour them on you. After not hearing what they want, the Love-Lorn tick will simply drop off somewhere.

If the hard line doesn't work and you still feel like you have to be there for your LUP, try setting time limits to his or her calls and visits. When the tick calls or stops by your home let it be known that you only have 15 minutes to listen to their problems. After their time is up, simply say that you have to leave on an imaginary errand. This should drive the tick off without snubbing them.

Another way of shaking off a tick is to visit their woods before they get to yours. If you want to be a good friend, go to their place and talk. This way you can leave on your own terms and your own conditions. Call them at work to talk, especially if you know they are busy. Give them a taste of their own medicine, innocently, of course. If this doesn't work, caller ID is available at most larger retail stores.

The Baby-sitter LUP

It's six o'clock on a Saturday night and it's your only night off work. You've got a big evening planned. Your date, who you've wanted to go out with for months, has made dinner reservations at an expensive French restaurant for eight o'clock to be followed by a night of dancing—and possibly more. Your floating on cloud nine. Unexpectedly, the doorbell rings. You hope it's your date arriving early, but to your disappointment, it's your sister. "Sis," she pleads, "I'm in a big bind. Will you watch Johnny and Susie for a 'few minutes' while I run to the store? I'll be right back. I promise."

At one o'clock the next morning your sister is pounding on the door yelling for you to let her in. You open the door and imaginary daggers pierce her body. Your date has long since excused himself from your impromptu plans and all you can think is Et tu Brute? You've spent your entire evening entertaining your sister's kids. You sacrificed your date, and a good movie on HBO for three hours of cartoons, twelve dollars on pizza, popcorn, and soda, and raised your blood pressure, all for her. "I'm so sorry" she cries. "I lost track of time and fell asleep on the couch. When I woke it was too late to get the kids and I didn't want to bother you."

Does this story, or a variation of it, sound familiar? To paraphrase an old adage, "If you can't screw your family and friends who can you screw?" Although friends can be ferocious Baby-sitter LUPs, family members are in a league by themselves. They are more terrifying because they are genetically linked and they know that guilt and a sense of obligation are sharp weapons in any arsenal. They also know that you would never jeopardize the well-being of their children because they are family. After

The Tick: "You wouldn't mind watching the kids for an hour, would you? I'll be right back."

all, blood is thicker than water—especially if it's your blood and their water.

Of course, accidents happen. But when they recur they are not accidents. They are premeditated schemes, whether the LUP realizes it or not. This philosophy may appear a little jaded, but when it comes to dealing with a Baby-sitter LUP it's all too often true.

Solutions

Bold-faced, preemptive lying is about the only way to deter the Baby-sitter LUP. Whenever they call, just tell them that you and/or your children have a very contagious case of the flu, and that you wouldn't want to expose their children to it. Naturally, you will be forced to stay home so you won't make a liar out of yourself when they catch you and the family eating out at a restaurant or enjoying a movie. Otherwise, lock your doors and bolt your windows because most family members will stop by in person to see if you're really sick. If you aren't, the feud between the Hatfield's and McCoys will seem like a church social. If that fails, charge your family $5.00 an hour to baby-sit and make them pay for the pizza. Bon Appetite!

The Job LUP

Time is money and money is time. Both are valuable and the Job LUP knows this. That's why he/she works hard at manipulating you to spend YOUR time doing THEIR job so THEY can make more money. This person not only monopolizes your time, which reduces your productivity, they also reap the benefits of your labor and selfishly accept all the credit. Whether it's the person who flashes a toothy smile and entices you to make copies for them "as long as you're at the copying machine" or the modern day Tom Sawyer who is always asking you to show them the "right way to paint a fence," everyone knows a Job LUP.

"When I was in the Army we had this guy in our unit from the hills of Kentucky who seemed like the dumbest guy on earth," said a friend from St Louis. "Whenever some unpleasant or difficult job came up he would suffer a memory lapse and forget how to do everything. Everybody else would end up doing his work for him. As soon as he got promoted to sergeant and didn't have to do the work himself, he remembered everything. Matter of fact, we found out later that he had one of the highest IQs in the entire company—

and we were in military intelligence! Hell, he was smarter than all of us put together!"

The "borrower" is another example or sub-breed of the Job LUP. This person basks in the thrill of borrowing pens, paper, tools, etc., and can be found sitting in a co-worker's chair with his/her feet propped up on their desk or drinking from a coffee cup other than their own. It's normally the same person who short-changes the coffee fund, forgets to bring a dish to the office party, skips their turn at cleaning up, and always arrives five minutes late for work and never gets reprimanded for it.

But the two worst breeds of Job or Office LUPs are the sycophant and the instigator. Both are a menace to the workplace and to society as a whole. The sycophant, a.k.a. the yes man or ass kisser, will appear to be trustworthy and friendly to co-workers, but once the boss appears their allegiance goes out the window. This person, along with the instigator, who delights in creating friction between co-workers and then steps aside like an innocent bystander, can't be trusted. They play the game, "Let's you and him fight."

> *"I worked in a newspaper office," lamented Karen from New York. "I had a co-worker who would always come to my desk and seem so interested in what I was doing and so willing to help. What she was actually doing was picking my brain for ideas and altering them slightly. She then presented them to the boss as her own. She got promoted and I didn't. I could have killed the bitch!"*

Solutions

The most difficult aspect of dealing with the plethora of Job LUPs is maintaining a good working environment and relationship. It would be easy to tell the Office LUP to "piss off," and to, "do their own work," but that method is not always practical. The Job LUP could quite possibly be your boss someday and just like the soldier from Kentucky, their memory could improve drastically and you could be on the corporate shit list. But all is not lost. Although the in-fighting can be cutthroat and bloody in most workplaces, it doesn't have to be. A little planning and subtle execution will do the trick. But it's always a tightrope act.

The first step in ridding your life of an Office LUP is to make yourself unavailable. That is, make it clear to them that you would be elated to help them with their work as soon as you finish yours. But the key is to appear like you never finish your work. If you can't get off the hook that way, graciously offer your help, but on your terms and on their time. Offer to help them during THEIR coffee break, during THEIR lunch, or after work. Since the Office LUP values their time more than yours, make them spend their time to get what they want. It may cost you a little extra effort in the beginning, but the tick will quickly grow weary of spending their free time and missing lunches, especially if they're free.

If you work at a profession where you use tools or office machinery and the LUP is constantly borrowing, simply set them up. Every time they borrow something, make sure that they sign a dated receipt and promise to return the tool and pay for any damage to it. After suffering through the embarrassment of returning your broken tools and the financial burden of replacing them, they won't be so quick to borrow them. This strategy works even better when tools and machinery are accountable items, such as at a factory or in many government jobs, and have to be checked out by hand-receipts. True, this is an inconvenient way to get an Office LUP off your back, but it's one of the best repellents on the market.

Freebie LUP

You have a special talent and ability—and everyone knows it. Whether you're a hairdresser, carpenter, doctor, electrician, lawyer, auto mechanic, writer, cook, seamstress, plumber, cop, or just have a strong back, your skill, expertise, and time are ripe for the picking. Mobs of salivating LUPs beat a path to your door and feed on your professional generosity and gullibility. As a friend or family member you are expected to offer your services free of charge. It goes with the territory. But excessive LUP behavior is annoying and consumes time in the short run and money in the long run. A lawyer doesn't attend school for seven years to give free advice and expect to repay school loans; a mechanic doesn't want to spend his or her free hours working on everyone else's car, nor is a hairdresser bound by a "law of the blood" contract which requires her to cut every familial hair free.

> *"I get so damned tired of cutting hair," said a stylist from Iowa. "I started out giving free haircuts to family and friends and that led into giving perms and other expensive treatments. Now I'm everybody's personal beautician. I should have never given that first free haircut. But now I don't have the heart to stop."*

With a little help anyone can learn to fight back. For instance, Wendy suffered from the same problem so acutely that she took a class in assertive training to learn to say NO to free haircuts from friends, family, neighbors, etc. With the help of the instructor, Frances, she gave herself an assignment to say NO to **anyone** who requested a free haircut. Frances, partly to challenge Wendy, and partly in fun, went to the beauty shop and said, "Wendy, I know about your assignment, but I wonder if you'd make an exception just this once. After all, I'm your instructor and friend...?" After a long pause, Wendy straightened up, waved her arms and belted out a triumphant, "NO."

Mike, a laborer from Illinois, stated, "I don't have any special skill, but I have a strong back and every time one of my friends moves they call and ask me to 'help them for an hour or two.' I don't mind carrying boxes and loading furniture, but I insist that they have everything packed and ready to be loaded when I arrive. It never works that way. When I get to their house nothing is boxed up and I spend my entire day wrapping and packing their dishes, silverware, nick-nacks, toys, picture frames, etc. Then I have to load it and help them clean up all the garbage they left around. I don't mind giving a few hours, but when it takes all my free time, it's a burden."

Solutions

When a freebie LUP attaches themselves to you the best way to shake them is to charge for your time. This doesn't mean if you're a physician and your LUP friend or brother comes knocking on your door with shooting pains in his left arm that you ask to be paid up front for your services. But it does mean that under normal circumstances you charge the LUP for your time and any expenses that you might incur. An effective method is to inform them ahead of time that you will "need" to begin charging a fee. It doesn't have to be your normal $50 an hour rate, but charging half should get the message across. By letting the LUP know this, you are setting conditions. If the LUP persists, reinforce your condition BEFORE you do anything. This will avoid any confusion and make them realize that you are serious.

Another tactic is to say "I don't have time right now. But if you come into my office, shop, or place of business, I should be able to work you in." Boom! Whistles blow, sirens wail, thunder rolls, and waves crash against the craggy rocks of their mind. Panic sets it. The LUP realizes that an "official" appointment means the "standard" rate for your services, and they don't want that. Their urgent plea of "I need your help," quickly fizzles down to a weak "I'll call you on Monday and let you know." The call will never come.

If by some genetic fault the parasite agrees to pay you "something," but it's not the amount you're asking for, use your judgment. Making a little extra money on the side doesn't hurt, and more important, you will have retained a friend and made a statement; that although your time might be cheap, it is not free.

The "I Don't Want To Be Alone LUP"

A lot of people hate to do anything alone. There's nothing abnormal about that. But when a person only uses another person to fill an empty seat in their car, or to accompany them while they push a grocery cart, it is not normal. They are ticks. How many people do you know that must have someone accompany them to a movie, a bar, restaurant, mall, or any other public place. In many cases, the Tick LUP doesn't care who's with them, as long as they have someone at their side. In fact, once they do, they often have their own agenda and pay little attention to whoever is accompanying them. The following account is an excellent example of "I Don't Want To Be Alone LUP" behavior:

> *"I have a female friend who only calls me when she wants to go out," said Lori, a professional salesperson. "I would agree to go out with her and as soon as we got to the dance club she'd be off in search of men. She would latch on to some guy and I would be left there alone. I wouldn't see her again until the bar closed. Sometimes, she'd leave with other people and*

I wouldn't hear from her again until the next time she wanted to go out. I was just somebody to fill a void. It didn't matter to her who she walked in with, she just didn't want to be alone."

Jack, a truck driver from Detroit, recalls a similar friend:

"I'm on the road five days a week and the last thing I want to do on my weekends is to travel. But I have a friend who can't go anywhere by himself. It seems that whenever he has to drive somewhere he calls me to ride along. He always says that he needs help doing a two-man job, but he doesn't need me. He just wants someone to ride with. Worse yet, he hardly talks during the trip. When he does talk, it's only about what he wants to talk about. When he's finished, he turns the radio up and ends the conversation. Finally, I stopped going anywhere with him. He'd be better off with a dog."

Solutions

The simplest method of plucking the "I Don't Want to be Alone" LUP from your scalp is not to set yourself up. Refuse to go out with them. But if for some masochistic reason you feel compelled to maintain this parasitic relationship, turn the tables in your favor by putting yourself in control of the situation. Take charge by offering to drive. This puts you in control, especially if you're going somewhere where the LUP is unable to leave you because they depend on you to get home. If he/she still insists on leaving you all to your lonesome, let them. Then leave them stranded. The message will come through loud and clear. A $40 taxi ride or an unscheduled night spent in a hotel will dissuade the most avid tick from sucking your time away.

This strategy costs them time AND money, and most likely the friendship of a loyal host. But the best method of avoiding the tick is to stay out of the forest.

TO DO LIST

1. In your journal, note when you are most often used and by whom. For example, by your best friend on week-ends, your family after work and on holidays, etc.
2. Identify how your time and/or professional expertise is being used.
3. Note how much time is being used by a LUP.
4. Place a value on your time, in either money or trade.
5. Begin charging for your time up front.
6. Use any money you earn to reward yourself. Purchase something you have always wanted, but have refused to spend money on.

4

THE LEECH

LEECH: A bloodsucking or carnivorous worm who preys on or clings to another.

The Leech is the most bloodthirsty and hard-to-kill LUP in the pantheon of parasites. The similarities between the Leech LUP and the parasite that it's named after are striking. Like the leech, the LUP is both male and female and is genetically engineered with suckers on both ends of its body. The Leech LUP has a far more voracious appetite than the other parasites we have examined thus far, for it feeds on possessions, time, money, and emotion. It creeps up on a victim innocently then strikes like an assassin--silent, swift, deadly. Once attached it hangs on for dear life.

The House Guest LUP

"I'll only stay a couple weeks until I find a place of my own and a new job. You won't even notice I'm here. I won't make a mess, I'll pay my share of the bills, I'll buy my own food, and I won't make any long distance calls." WARNING, WARNING, DANGER, DANGER! Pull up, bail out, and run for your life. A LUP is about to invade your home and body and deliver a bloody *coup de main* to your pocketbook. This cancerous plea has destroyed more friendships than any line since "Trust Me" or "The Check is in the Mail." The situation is even worse with family. When 30 year-old "children" refuse to leave the nest or keep returning to it to avoid paying rent and utilities, buying food, doing laundry, or assuming independence, they are more than parasites, they are lazy parasites.

Like a master carpenter, the House Guest LUP uses the parasitic tools of its trade and hammers at your heart, paints a rosy picture of living together, and screws you blind—whether they know it or not. With a full-time live-in "mia casa--sua casa" will take on an entirely new meaning. So, if you're dying to get stuck with astronomical utility bills, get eaten out of house and home, sacrifice your privacy, clean up someone else's messes, tolerate a steady flow of strangers through your door, forfeit your favorite easy chair, share the remote control, elevate your blood pressure, and lose your emotional well-being, invite a house guest LUP into your home.

> *"I had a friend from work who left her abusive boyfriend and needed a place to stay," said Mindy, a waitress from Illinois. "She promised that she would only stay a couple of weeks until she found a place. She gave me a little money here and there for rent, but she lost her job right after she moved in. She didn't pay me a dime after that. I didn't have the heart to kick her out, but I went broke supporting both of us. To make matters worse, she didn't even look for a job. After three months I moved out! I made a big mistake by leting her move in and I'm still paying for it."*

"My former college roommate screwed me real good!"
added Tom, a business man from northern Ohio. "A two-
day friendly visit turned into a two-month adoption. I
kept urging him to find a job and he would always tell
me that he was interviewing for one, but he would never
get hired. When I would come home from work he'd be
lying on the couch watching television or talking on the
phone. I finally booted his ass out. But he got the last
laugh. He left me with a $200 phone bill!"

Solutions

Besides posting a well-lit "No Vacancy" sign in your window, the only way to deter the House Guest LUP is to NEVER let them in. They will consume you. If by some lapse in judgment, or an infliction of temporary insanity, you invite such a creature into your home, there are a few strategies available. But understand that there is NO easy solution, especially when family is involved.

As with lesser parasites, it's necessary to poison the blood if you want to rid yourself of the Leech LUP. It must become your sole mission to make their life miserable and to make them WANT to leave. Ideally, the first step would be to set absolute conditions on the length of their stay BEFORE they move in. But the LUP knows this and is quick to pre-empt the host by volunteering that their stay will be brief. As the host it is necessary to counter with "You can stay until such and such time" and then I'll have to charge you so much up front for rent, utilities, food, etc. After that point I expect x amount of dollars on such and such date." Do not accept the common sidestep of "I'll help out." Set monetary amounts. It's also a good idea to draw up a contract and make the LUP accept legal responsibility for any long distance calls they make and for half of the rent and utilities. They may act hurt that you would question their integrity by requiring a contract, but have them sign it.

Second, establish strict rules. Make it clear that your home is yours not theirs. Make them feel like they are living at home with

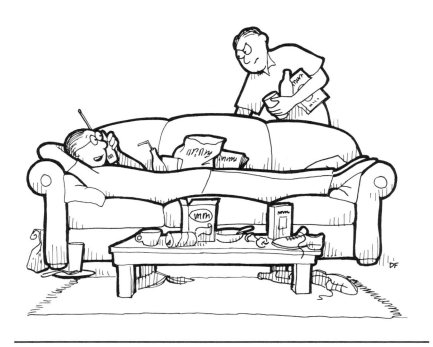

The Leech: "I am looking for my own place. . . I'm calling right now!"

their parents again, that is if they aren't already. Constant bitching about everything under the sun adds a nice touch of realism, as does a steady flow of housework and a curfew. Waking the LUP up from a sound sleep early every morning to "share your feelings" is another oldie but goodie. When that doesn't work, starve them out. Buy fewer groceries each time you go shopping or buy food for yourself and hide it in your bedroom. Once the feedbag begins drying up, they should get the hint. Also, under no circumstances allow them to use your vehicle...unless it's to move!

Third, consider inviting someone the LUP detests, but you like and trust, to "move in for a few days." Of course, brief the new guest on all the behaviors that annoy the LUP. That will take the onus off you and put the heat on the LUP to relocate. But be careful, there is always the possibility that they may become friends and then you will have to move!

If none of these strategies is effective, and it seems that you will forever have to claim an extra person on your tax return, it's time to play hardball. Simply make them leave. You will probably ruin the friendship—but, if it's strictly a host/parasite relationship, you don't need it anyway.

The I Love You LUP (Romantic)

Everyone loves to be loved one way or the other. But when breathing the rarefied air of *amore* it's often impossible to get enough oxygen to our brains to see an "I Love You LUP" racing toward our hearts at mach 2 with suckers blazing! What makes this parasite so lethal is that it rarely strikes until it and the victim have uttered those "three magic words" and surrendered all sensibility. By that time neither the host nor the LUP can distinguish loving from lupping. Most horrifying is that the LUP often doesn't realize that they are using the one they love. It is this fine-line definition which separates the Leech from the calculating Vampire described in the next chapter.

The Leech believes that being "in love" is a mandate to manipulate, suffocate, and subjugate, but seldom donate. This truest of parasites is insatiable. It strikes first at the heart then usurps the victim's time, freedom, and possessions. It's feeding is so ravenous that it ultimately consumes the love which sustained it. Guilt is the leeches' weapon of choice. Such razor sharp contritions as "If you really loved me you would ..." or "People who love each other ..." inflict gaping wounds upon the host and compel them to give into the LUP's demands—all in the name of love.

Time is a tasty appetizer in an "I Love You LUP's" feast.

"I met a beautiful woman who was just too good to be true," recalled Dave, a policeman from California. "Our relationship was great until we said that we loved each other. From that moment she took more and more of my

time until she had it all. The moment I walked in the door from work she would call. Then she would show up ten minutes later uninvited and expect me to cancel my plans. If I didn't she would go berserk and scream "you don't love me." She made me feel guilty and I would alter my plans to suit her. One night I went out of town to visit family and when I returned I had 14 messages on my answering machine. On some of them she talked nicely and on others she screamed and accused me of being with another woman. I felt like I had a ball and chain on me. Her time was her time and my time was her time. She was too good to be true. I don't know why I put up with her."

And for the first course...your possessions.

"I must have sucker stamped on my forehead" said Angela, an account executive from Georgia. "The last relationship I was involved in started out fine, but the closer my boyfriend and I got, the more he began acting like he owned me. During a weak moment I gave him the key to my apartment and before I knew it he was coming over and doing his laundry, cooking meals, and using whatever I had like it was his own. We had different work schedules and I would often come home and find him in my apartment. If I didn't arrive at my usual time he would begin grilling me about where I had been. Then I began noticing that little things were missing from my apartment and that he had gone through my personal papers and old love letters, and such. I felt violated and I told him so, but he would just say that he loved me and dismiss it. Like a fool, I rationalized his behavior. But it got to the point where he controlled every facet of my life. After wasting a year with him, I finally woke up. I removed my key from his key ring while he was sleeping. The next day I left on a two-week vacation to the Bahamas."

The Parental I Love You Card—
We won't leave home without it!

And for the piece de resistance . . . money!

"I developed a relationship with a lady from a nearby town and once we got serious her behavior changed," said Al, a contractor in a small midwestern town. "On more than one occasion she asked me over for dinner, but she wouldn't have any food. She would then ask if I would drive to the market and buy whatever I wanted to eat. I didn't mind the first couple times, but like an idiot I wound up buying her groceries on a regular basis. After doing that for her a few times she suddenly moved to the same apartment complex that I lived in without telling me. That's when she really got to me. She started making excuses to come over all the time. Either her television was broken, or it was too cold in her apart-

55

ment, or she didn't feel safe. It was always something. She had a young child and would use him to soften me up for the kill. She would say that he needed this or that and then ask me to loan her money for rent, or to pay bills, or to buy something the kid needed. She usually put the touch on me right after we had sex. She would begin crying and I couldn't stand it. I can't believe I fell for it. I even let her borrow my credit card one time to use only in case of an emergency while she went out of state for job training. Thirty-five hundred dollars and one helluva shopping spree later I got it back. It's embarrassing to even talk about. I was blinded by love and I paid for it. The sad thing is that we had a wonderful relationship in the beginning, but she felt that love was a license to use and abuse."

Solutions

Everyone gets bitten by the Love LUP bug at least once. Sometimes it's only a mild sting, other times it's a fat, red welt. Regardless of the severity, affairs of the heart often leave us vulnerable and exposed. The adage "an ounce of prevention is worth a pound of cure," is priceless advice when dealing with the I Love You LUP. A potent dose of emotional repellent, applied liberally during the first month of a relationship, is the best way to prevent a LUP siege. This life-saving concoction should include the following ingredients:

Recipe for I Love You LUP Repellent

- 1 Bushel of Common Sense
- 1 Pound of Birth Control
- 1 Medium Brain
- 1 Heart (Chilled or Hardened)
- A Measure of Reality
- A Pinch of Skepticism

- A dash of Reason
- A Jigger of Awareness
- And 1 Trustworthy Countersigner for all financial transactions

Blend ingredients with experience, intuition, and hindsight. Season to taste with understanding and tact. Vigorously rub mixture on sensitive areas, such as heart, soul, mind, wallet or purse. Repeat steps as necessary. Serves everyone.

Of course, this recipe for repellent is only effective when applied BEFORE the I Love You LUP has acquired a taste for your blood type. Getting rid of them AFTER they're attached to you demands a more lethal prescription—POISON! Not real poison, but an emotional bane so virulent that it forces the LUP to either drop off or die.

Love is the core of the I Love You LUPs' existence and the rationale for their parasitic behavior. They want it. They need it. They have to have it. An I Love You LUP without love is akin to an arsonist without matches. They are harmless. Therefore, to take the blood out of their bellies you must take the love out of your heart.

Don, a factory worker from Missouri, explains how he rid himself of an I Love You LUP:

"When I finally had enough of being used I began detaching myself emotionally, physically, and financially. I had tried to end our relationship cold turkey, but the sudden split was too hard for her to take. She kept hounding me and I began feeling sorry for her, so I took her back. I realized that the only way I could get rid of her and live in peace was to make her leave me. It was a war of attrition. I began denying her sexually. This frustrated her terribly. Next, I quit doing little favors like buying flowers and gifts and taking her out to eat. I also started

spending most of my free time away from the house and I quit giving her money and supporting her. Basically, I made excuses for everything and blamed everyone else for our deteriorating relationship. That kept her off my back. After a while I could tell that she felt that the relationship was dying out. She made several last gasp efforts at holding on to me by 'manufacturing' all sorts of major crises. I fell for a couple, which cost me money, but it didn't take long for me to realize that they were just ploys. Finally, she couldn't take my disinterest in her and in her problems. She left blaming me. I didn't care anymore. I was just glad that she was gone."

The I Love You LUP (Family)

Few things in life are more satisfying than having your children say "I love you..." and mean it unconditionally. On the other hand, nothing is more painful than knowing that "I love you mom or I love you dad" is only a tender trap for snaring money or a new car. Parents expect to hand out money and buy things for their children, while children expect to receive them. Every parent wants what is best for their children and they try to make their lives as comfortable as possible, but parents often overcompensate by giving and doing too much for them. This subsidizes leech behavior and frequently nurtures a life-long dependent. But remember, its important to distinguish genuine need and family give-and-take from blood letting. It's normal and accepted that family stops by during meals or that it's okay for children in college to come home on weekends with two baskets of dirty laundry and no money in their pockets.

"You know when your 21-year-old son says 'I love you, dad' that he's wanting money," said John. "He hasn't said that to me since he was 10 years old. It's funny that every time his car breaks down or when he needs money for college he loves me!"

"Like most parents, I co-signed an automobile loan for my daughter so she would have transportation at college," recalled Cindy, a mother of three. "She promised me that she would get a part-time job and make the payments. When she got to college all she could find time for was socializing. She skipped three payments in a row and the bank called and warned me that if I didn't catch up on the payments they would repossess the car and that my credit rating would be ruined. A couple months after I made the payments she blew the engine up in the car. Now she's walking, but I still have to make a payment once in a while. I learned my lesson."

"I always knew that mom would take care of me," said Greg, a 36-year-old LUP. "Even though I worked and could afford my own place, I lived with my mom until last year. I saved money that way and had plenty to spend on whatever I wanted. She would buy my cigarettes and groceries, clean the house, give me extra money when I needed it, and do my wash. I sometimes gave her a little money when she asked. There was no reason for me to get my own place. Why should I? Mom was doing everything for me and I let her. I loved her but used her every chance I got. Finally out on my own I realize how much of a burden I was, but I still go to her house everyday for lunch and sometimes dinner."

But leech lupping isn't confined only to children. Parents, brothers, sisters, aunts, uncles, cousins, in-laws, and long-lost shirt-tail relations are equally cunning. No one knows better than family which guilt buttons to push. They know your strengths, your weaknesses, and how best to, knowingly or unknowingly, manipulate you to get what they want. Family members are notorious for luring each other into fly-by-night business ventures, most of which cost the host more money than the LUP. Conventional wisdom dictates that "if you want to get screwed, go into business with family." How true.

"My brother talked me into investing in a restaurant,"
said Nicole. "He said that he would take care of every-
thing. All I had to do was front the down payment and
share in the profit. He was half right. I invested money,
but I didn't share any profit, not at first anyway. Actu-
ally, he was more enchanted with owning a business than
operating one. The only thing I shared in was the labor.
I ended up running the place full time, and I knew noth-
ing about the restaurant business. He moved out of town
and took a sales job and I had to either step in or sell the
business for a loss."

"I owned a successful bar in Kentucky," said Craig.
"My dad was near retirement and wanted to get involved
in business with me. I thought it would be a great chance
to spend some time with him and that it would give him
something productive to do. So, I let him buy one-third
interest in the bar. He nearly broke me! He was inviting
all his drinking buddies in and giving them free drinks,
the expensive stuff! Every time he gave away a drink he
cost me money. When I said something to him about it,
he flew off the handle and accused me of not knowing
how to run a business. Not only that, my brothers and
sisters began turning on me because I was being so hard
on him. I became the damn black sheep of the family for
trying to help him out! Lucky for me, he got bored with
the whole thing and sold his share back to me. That's
the last time I ever go into business with anyone from
my family."

Solutions

See "Recipe for I Love You LUP " Repellent (Relationship)," and triple the ingredients. Substitute birth control with a firm "NO" and serve ice cold!

Free Lunch LUP

The focus of this work centers on the dynamic of the individual host-parasite relationship rather than on the nature of broader parasitic feeding habits, but something must be said about the Free Lunch LUP, better known as the "Take Care of Me Leech." This critter possesses the innate ability to live off institutions rather than individuals. Every community has its share. They are the able-bodied and able-minded people who use, abuse, and defraud government, religious, and civic institutions because it's easier and more profitable than working. These bloodsuckers play the welfare system like a cheap piano and make it more difficult for those who legitimately need and deserve assistance to receive it. The behavior not only burdens the taxpayers but drains them of compassion for the truly unfortunate.

"I use the government every chance I get," said Keith, a single 37-year-old LUP. "I receive food stamps, full housing assistance, Medicaid, and social security assistance from the government, and clothing, food, and other benefits from local churches and from the YMCA. I sell the food stamps for 50 cents on the dollar and sublet one of the rooms in my apartment to a friend. I work odd jobs for cash every chance I get. When I need more money, I get a real job and work for a while. Then I always get hurt on the job and collect workman's commensation insurance and unemployment. I'll keep doing it as long as the government lets me."

"I make more money from the government by not working," added Lana. "Why work every day for minimum

wage, when I can make the same amount by not working at all. It would be stupid for me to go to work. I live with my boyfriend and he works. As long as we don't get married I'll keep receiving a check."

Solutions

No free lunches.

TO DO LIST

1. In your journal, list the name of the Leeches you have supported in your life and how they have used you. Look for common "soft spots." Are you a sucker for family members who are short on money? Do you get satisfaction from being someone's romantic "savior?" Identify what it is about your personality that is vulnerable.

2. Ask other people what they see as your weaknesses. Compare how you see yourself and how others see you.

3. Every day try to learn more about yourself and how to read people. Be alert for Leech warning signs. Look at other people and their leeches. Be objective and compare their behavior with your's and your leech. Look for similarities and differences.

4. Develop a strategy and a timetable for ridding yourself of your leech. Eliminate one host behavior a week until you wean yourself from your leech. Begin by saying "no" to at least one commom leech request a week.

5. Be aware of lurking leeches and how you can discourage them before they attach themselves.

6. Reward yourself for your anti-leech behavior by spending more time with nurturing friends.

Losers, Users & Parasites

5

THE VAMPIRE

VAMPIRE: (1) One who sucks the blood of others. (2) One who preys upon others, as: a. An extortionist. b. A woman or man who uses sexual attraction to exploit the opposite sex.

The Vampire is the most terrible, frightening, and ruthless parasite in existence, for it has no soul. This evil creature targets its prey and captivates them with its charms. Once it has the victim under its spell, the vampire bears its teeth and sinks them deep into the victim's financial jugular. After it has gorged itself, it disappears into the night and leaves its victim for dead. Do real vampires exist? No. But LUPs do, and what better sobriquet for the cold, calculating LUP than the "vampire."

Unlike other parasites, the Vampire LUP is fully aware of its "need to feed," and is simply out for personal gain. This amoral fiend is without conscience and is unencumbered by feelings of guilt and remorse. Whether its money, power, fame, prestige, or a combination of the above, the Vampire is a cold-blooded user and will stop at nothing to obtain what it wants. What makes this parasite so lethal is that it masks its true colors like a chameleon and changes into whatever the host (target) NEEDS or DESIRES it to be. The Vampire is an astute judge of character and a virtuoso at plucking its host's emotional, physical, or spiritual strings. Like a Godsend, the Vampire magically fills a void in its victim's life and endears itself to its prey. By dropping their guard and allowing the vampire to do this, the host is simply "inviting the biting."

In the Host Test in Chapter one you recall that having a lot of money doesn't necessarily mean that you would make a good host, only a good target. Keep that in mind while reading more about the vampire LUP.

The Gold Digger LUP

You don't have to be a millionaire, a Hollywood movie star, or a professional athlete to get bitten by a vampire. Wealth is relative. Just as there are many different levels of wealth, there are also many levels of Gold Digging LUPs. Some pursue billionaires while others pursue John or Jane Doe off the street. Regardless of the number of zeros in their bank accounts or the particular metallic color of their credit cards, each host has something to offer the vampire. It's up to the individual vampire to decide whose blood is rich enough for their taste. Gold diggers are often stereotyped as young, beautiful women. But women do not have the market cornered when it comes to gold digging. Men are just as cunning. Gender means nothing when its "Love at First Bite."

"I inherited a substantial amount of money," explained Kathy, a 45-year-old woman living in the Midwest. "I'm not a physically attractive person and I had never been married. But as soon as I received my inheritance I had men coming out of the woodwork. One particular man, who was very handsome, swept me off my feet. He said and did all the right things. He bought me flowers, took

me dancing, and treated me like a queen. When I was around him I felt like the most beautiful woman in the world. We dated for about three months and got married. That's when he began taking charge of all the finances. He spent money like it was going out of style, but I didn't really care. I was happy for the first time in my life. A year later he served divorce papers on me. It was then that I discovered that he had swindled me out of several thousand dollars. I'm talking six figures! Now I don't trust anyone. It was a hard lesson."

"As soon as the money was gone, she was gone," said Jack, a farmer from Iowa. "At one time I had a large farming operation and a lot of land. This young woman kept showing up wherever I was and she eventually introduced herself. She was uncommonly beautiful and it didn't take me long to become interested in her. We began seeing each other regularly and we developed a great relationship. Frankly, the woman lured me in with sex. She kept my head spinning and I lost all judgment. She kept hinting around for me to ask her to move in, and I did. Then she wanted a new car. I said "fine." Then there was all the jewelry. She was making me happy and I felt that she genuinely loved me, so I didn't mind buying her expensive things and giving her money like it was candy. Then, the farming business went to hell and I lost my ass. One day I came home from work and she was gone, along with the car, the jewelry, and some valuables of mine. She left a note saying that 'she just couldn't take it anymore.' The bitch had it planned all along! I was heartbroken at first, but then I got mad."

Mavis, a secretary from a small town in Indiana, recalls: "There was a lonely old man who lived down the street from my sister and me. He didn't have any family and we used to go to his house and visit with him. It's sad to say, but we used this guy. He bought our company. He would buy us whatever we wanted as long as we kept coming over. Whenever we needed money or new clothes or whatever, we would just flirt with him and he'd give us what we wanted. We led him on. I never had sex with him, but I suspect that my sister did. I know that he bought her a new car and that he spent a lot of money on her. She even got him to amend his will and to include her in it. If it wasn't for his money, we wouldn't have given him the time of day."

Solutions

There are two ways to drive a stake through the heart of a gold digging, Vampire LUP. One is to be proactive and to protect yourself before you get bitten. Short of wearing a garlic necklace, a body-sized crucifix, and going out in public only in daylight, about all you can do is be on guard. Trust your instincts and intelligence, not your heart. If scores of dream lovers suddenly materialize at the same time your net worth does, be careful. According to legend, the vampire does not cast a reflection in a mirror. This can be interpreted in two ways. First, that it is able to approach and bite its victim from behind, even if the victim is looking in a mirror. This is clearly to the advantage of the vampire. The second is that the vampire casts no reflection because it doesn't have a soul. This is to the advantage of the potential victim. Therefore, its important to carry a mirror and to be vigilant. In other words, find out if the potential vamp has a soul.

At the expense of dulling the luster of true love, you should hold up a few mirrors in front of the suspected vampire LUP and subtlety ask the following questions:

1. What single characteristic do you like best about me?
2. How would you feel if I quit my job and went back to school?
3. What was best and worst about your last few relationships?

4. Which three people besides family do you admire the most and why?
5. What single thing besides love would make you happiest?

It doesn't take a degree in Sigmund Freud and hours of psychoanalysis to gain a little insight into a person from their answers. Simply look for consistencies. If the questionable LUP likes your generosity, doesn't want you to return to school, loved their ex's mansion in Bel Air, would be forever happy not working, and unabashedly admires John D. Rockefeller, Donald Trump, and Robin Givens, it's time to break out another clove of garlic and don an iron turtleneck.

As long as you have a mirror handy, you might also want to peer into it for a little self-reflection. Remember, trust your instincts and intelligence, not your heart. Be as cold-blooded and emotionless as the vampire when answering these questions.

- What void does this person fill in my life?
- Does this person work overtime to fill that void?
- What do I have to gain from this relationship?
- What do I have to lose?
- What does this person have to gain?
- Were they better off financially before of after we met?
- Does this relationship center around money and things?
- Is this relationship costing me a lot of money?
- Do I buy everything of value?
- Does this person "trade" their time and affection for things of value?
- Does this person use sex to soften me up?
- What does their past tell about them?

If the bottom line doesn't add up and leaves you in the red-- blood red, it's time to re-evaluate your relationship. Vampire LUPs don't hold up very well under the glaring light of day. The other

The Vampire: "I love you for YOU!"

way of getting rid of a vampire LUP is less appetizing. For either you get rid of them before they bite you, or they bite you first and get rid of you. Once you've been bitten there is little you can do except to learn from the experience and take steps to insure that you don't set yourself up as a tasty snack for the next LUP that flashes a toothy grin. The unpleasant experience may have cost you a lot of time, money, and heartache, but life goes on. Next time, consider a pre-nuptial agreement.

Scam LUP

Why do Vampire LUPs con, swindle, cheat, and steal? What drives this heartless parasite to expend great energy in scamming others when they could just as easily make an honest living with the same effort? Why do powerful nations conquer weak ones when they have little to gain? Why do some people spend $5,000 for a bottle of wine? Why does a person climb Mt. Everest? These and other great mysteries of life have perplexed philosophers, sages, and common man for thousands of years. Without looking for the higher meaning of existence, the answer is simple, and can be found by observing man's best friend. Yes, that's right, the dog.

What does a dog have to do with why a Scam LUP delights in duping? Easy. Why does a dog lick itself? **BECAUSE IT CAN!** With all due respect to Plato and Confucius, who are probably turning over in their graves, this crude, but timeless philosophy, is basic to the Scam LUP. They feast on human gullibility and are nourished by the pleasant feeling, sense of power, and superiority they derive from their actions. A man, who was probably a Scam Artist, once said "Whenever you find a fool, make a fool out of him every time you find him." So much for higher meaning.

Several species of Scam LUPs exist, most of them in the business world. Once one successfully sinks their teeth into a victim, others surely follow. Like other parasites, Vampire LUPs are expert networkers and will pass along the name and location of any free-flowing blood banks to other LUPs, so they too can make a withdrawal. According to one's perception, fortune tellers, insurance agents, telemarketers, shell-game operators, snake-oil salesmen, used car dealers, attorneys, and even Uncle Sam might easily qualify as vampires. It's up to the individual to decide which one, if any, fits into this category. Listed below are a few examples.

"I received a phone call from an aluminum siding salesman," said Paul, a retiree from Minnesota. "All the person wanted to know is if they could stop by and show me some samples. The cost of the siding was so inexpensive that I couldn't pass it up. He undercut every contractor in the area by a great deal. All the salesman required was a $1000 deposit to get the job going. He asked me if any of my friends needed siding and I gave him their names. He sold a couple of them on it too. Two weeks went by and I didn't hear a word from him. I called around and discovered that the company he said that he worked for didn't even exist."

"I got taken to the cleaners by someone I thought was a friend," said Larry, a large livestock broker from the Midwest. "I sold several hundred head of cattle to a guy and by law he could take them home and was allowed three days to pay for them. The day after he picked up the cattle he sold them to another man and filed bankruptcy. I got screwed real good! I found out later that he did the same thing to two or three other guys."

"Our insurance man seemed like the nicest person," said an elderly couple from central Illinois. "He would always call on us and drop by just to say hello. Little did we know that he was scoping out our house for valuables. Several other clients told him that they were going to Florida for the winter. It turned out that he was stealing antiques, jewelry, and other valuables from us and from other people while we were on vacation. People began putting two and two together. He was eventually caught and sent to prison. His house was full of stolen property. He had everyone conned into believing that he was their friend. He got what he deserved."

Solutions

Keep in mind two wise sayings: "If it seems too good to be true, it probably is," and "Caveat Emptor—buyer beware!" Common Sense, suspicion, and restraint are the greatest repellents in fending off the Scam LUP. Avoid impulse buying. If what the Scam LUP is trying to sell or convince you to do is valid "today only," don't believe it. Question, question, and re-question them. In other words, interrogate.

If you suspect that the person is a vampire and is filing their teeth in anticipation of a quick kill, smash them in the mouth. Ask for proof of their product or service. Call the Better Business Bureau. Ask for the names and phone numbers of the corporate office, their immediate supervisor, and of satisfied clients. Then call the local police and inquire if there has been any con man activity reported in your area. After all that's complete, ask the salesperson to leave some literature and to return in two weeks. If they really want to make a sale they'll be back. In the meantime, continue your own investigation.

In the event that you are a bleeder, apply direct pressure and a sterile dressing, and chalk it up to experience. You've been had. Score one for the vampire.

Salvation LUP

The Salvation LUP is the lowest form of parasite on the planet, but also the most savage. What separates this invasive breed of vampire from other vampires is that it targets the masses, not specific individuals. That's right, you guessed it, televangelists! The Elmer Gantrys of the world. By no means is this an indictment of all them, but there are those (and they shall be known by their works) who have violated the public trust by bilking their victims out of millions of dollars in the name of religion. These parasitic monsters prey (pardon the pun), on the spiritual lifeblood of their believers, many of whom are poor and elderly, and coerce them into believing that the only way to receive salvation is to buy it—from them. While the vampires grow fat on tithes, their victims often deprive themselves of the basic necessities of life.

Knowing that everyone has erred, the vampire rattles the skeletons in it's victim's closet and makes them believe that they must atone for their "sinful past" by buying limited edition dinner plates of the Last Supper or some cheap imitation crystal manufactured by atheists in Taiwan, the proceeds from which often pay for the vampire's luxury car, summer home, or air conditioned dog house.

When guilt doesn't draw the necessary amount of blood, some vampires play the fear card. This can be anything from fear of eternal damnation to the fear end of the world to the fear of "God calling them home." All the host has to do is to send money to the vampire and the fear will evaporate...drop by drop, pint by pint, dollar by dollar.

"For years I gave to one television ministry," lamented Marge. "I was unable to attend church, so I watched religious programming from my home. I sent every spare dollar I could. Then the demands got heavier. The ministry began sending additional requests through the mail asking me to give more. They would also send little gifts thanking me for my faith. They made me feel guilty, so I began dipping into my savings. My children were very angry at me and warned me not to send so much money. Then all these reports came out about what this man was actually doing with the money. It was going into his pocket, not into the church. I felt hurt and deceived. I spent most of my savings and now I'm soured on religion. I still have my faith, but it's getting harder to believe in anything anymore."

"I can't believe that I fell for it!" said George, referring to his bequest of several thousand dollars to a popular television ministry. "I had it arranged that when I died a substantial sum of money would go to a specific preacher and to his church. But the preacher had a fall from grace and they canceled the show. Therefore, I canceled my bequest. I couldn't believe some of the things that he was doing. All along I thought that I had led a wicked life. Mine doesn't compare."

Solutions

The best medicine available for dealing with the Salvation LUP is knowledge and information. Before you commit your pocketbook to them, make them commit to you. Request in writing a financial statement and detailed account of how and where your money will be spent. Do a little digging and inquire how much the "priceless gift" that you will receive for your donation costs them to manufacture. Since most ministries are tax-exempt they should be eager to provide a statement showing how they didn't make a profit. If your efforts meet with great resistance, assume that you will be nailed to the old rugged cross.

It is not until unscrupulous vampires have been exposed for what they really are—hypocritical parasites who feed off the blood of others, that they are killed. Unfortunately, the damage is already done and some vampires return from the dead. Because of the biting they received many believers become disillusioned with their faith. Like Dracula's victims, they too are left drained, bitter, and spiritually dead.

The key to surviving the bite of a salvation LUP is to understand that it was the manipulation OF your faith, BY the vampire, FOR their benefit, not the fault of a particular religion, most of which are centered around truth and espouse virtuous existence.

TO DO LIST

1. Understand that everything is not always as it appears to be. People have ulterior motives when dealing with you.
2. Be realistic. If something appears to good to be true...Beware, both personally and professionally.
3. Minimize your chances of getting bitten by a vampire by realizing that you are a potential target to someone, regardless of what you believe you may or may not have.
4. Do not give trust away--force others to earn it.

6

FLEAS, FLIES, & OTHER PESTS

A plethora of bloodsucking parasites have been exposed throughout this book that lurk in the shadows waiting to dine on human dejour. You are now more aware of their existence and how to avoid becoming a main course. Although you may feel impenetrable to parasitic attacks, you are still vulnerable to another form of attack—that of the pest. Pests, otherwise known by the nom de guerres "solicitor, telemarketer, and salesman," assault you in the relative safety and privacy of your home and cannibalize your free time. Unless you are unable to say no to anything, pests are usually harmless, but their relentless barrage is maddening.

Consider the following scenario:

You come home after a hard day on the job and sit down for a relaxing dinner. Before you are able to get the first bite into your salivating mouth the telephone rings. An unfamiliar voice quickly greets you and launches into a rapid sales spiel. The person is trying to sell you a home security system, travel insurance, credit card protection, stocks, investments, or even gold. Or maybe its a telemarketer: (Flea) from a long-distance telephone company, the one you just switched from, promising the world, along with a $5 rebate, if you reinstate their company as your long-distance provider.

Even more horrifying, it's the local law enforcement agency (other pest) asking you to donate to the "policeman's benevolent fund again this year," when you only moved into town a month ago. In return for a donation, they promise to send you a decal for your car which shows the world what a great citizen you are, a decal which you hope will bail you out of a speeding ticket someday. So, you agree to donate.

After selling out for fear of appearing on a police hit list, you hang up. Suddenly, there's a knock at the front door. You grudgingly answer it. A salesman (fly) dressed in a cheap, ill-fitting polyester suit and a fake smile stands before you attempting to get his large foot in the door. Following a brief verbal scuffle from which you emerge bloody but unbowed, you return to the table and attempt to consume what once was a piping hot dinner.

Halfway through your meal the doorbell rings. "This had better be important," you grumble, as the veins in your neck become more prominent. You answer the door while still chewing a tepid piece of roast beef. To your surprise two young, well-dressed gentlemen ask if you believe in heaven. Suddenly, the terror registers on your face like a trapped rat eating cheese. Ten minutes and a half dozen "amens" later, you're free to return to dinner.

You finish a cold meal and retire to the easy chair for an evening of relaxation in front of the television. Fifty-five minutes into your favorite one-hour mystery, the telephone rings again. "Damn!" you cry, hoping against hope that it's not another telemarketer. No such luck. You abruptly cut them off, but it's too late. The program is over. The culprit has been exposed and you are left trying to figure out just whodunit.

A little extreme possibly, but in today's fast-paced lifestyle and global economy, more and more businesses, civic and religious organizations, have turned to the telephone and to direct home sales to market their products and services or to spread their respective messages.

Naturally, they are unable to target the general public at their workplace. So, they target them at home. This translates into more irritation, less quiet time, and an irate public who is sick and tired of being harassed at home. For many people, especially those with manners, it is nearly impossible to hang up on a telemarketer or solicitor, or to coldly dismiss a salesman at the front door. If you're one of those people, the next few pages will be of great interest to you.

The Flea

Technically, the flea is also a parasite, but for the purposes of this chapter, it is simply a pest—a large one! Thus, what better name to give telemarketers than the flea. The flea is a major annoyance and serious health risk. Contrary to popular belief, rats weren't responsible for the bubonic plague which wiped out one third of the population of Europe in the 13th century. It was the fleas who lived on the rat that were responsible! Therefore, if fleas are eliminated, so is the plague, which in the case of this work is defined as irritation. If you are one of the millions of people whose home is infested with fleas and whose body is ridden with the modern day plague, take heart. There is hope. The following are a few simple and fun remedies that will get the most diehard flea off your back.

Telephone Solicitor Call

If a telephone solicitor's call is an unwanted intrusion, just say, "Not interested. Thank you just the same." And hang up. Studies report that some people can't get off the phone even when they know they're being drawn into a scam!

If the caller is some one who you don't want to antagonize unnecessarily (Police Benefit), it's considered assertive—not aggressive--to give three warnings, like " I have to leave now," or

"I'm sorry, I have no more time to talk, so I have to hang up," and do it.

Solutions

Only a rude hang-up will shake a flea off the phone faster than making them believe that they have reached the wrong number. Upon hearing their potential victim's voice, the flea will immediately ask, "Is this Mr/Mrs. (your name)." Beat them to the punch and forcefully answer "No, it isn't. You nave the wrong number." But be careful, they may call back. If so, don't answer the phone. Here's a little tip to ferret out most fleas. If your name is difficult to pronounce and the caller butchers it badly, chances are it's someone who doesn't know you personally.

Another method of dusting off an unwanted telemarketer is to lie! We've all done it. When the caller reveals what their purpose is, assume that same purpose. For example, if they're selling insurance, interrupt them immediately and say that you're also an insurance agent and that you sell the same product that they do. After a brief apology, the flea will hang up and search for another target.

If lying is morally repugnant to you and abruptly hanging up is out of the question, try avoidance. Place the receiver next to the stereo, tune in on a heavy metal song, turn up the volume (real loud), and walk away. No more flea!

The most effective and enjoyable method of getting rid of a telemarketer flea is role reversal. As soon as the person introduces theirself and their intention, enthusiastically proclaim, "I'm glad you called. I have something I want to sell you!" With utmost ruthlessness take the offensive and start selling the five hundred head of live hogs you've been wanting to market. Ignore the stuttering on the other end of the line and ask THEM for their credit card number and where to deliver the screaming swine. The tables will be turned and they will be trying to get off the phone with you! Try it, it's fun!

Door To Door Pest

Another irksome pest is the door-to-door salesperson or the fly. It is so named because whenever a door is left open, even for a millisecond, the pesky creature dashes into your house and annoys you until it is either crushed or decides to leave under its own propulsion. Unlike telemarketers, who can either be politely or rudely dismissed over the anonymity of a telephone, door-to-door salespeople are not as easy to dispose of—for you see their face—and they see yours. Such intimate encounters weaken many people's defenses, particularly if the solicitor has a pleasant personality or is physically attractive. After the initial surprise of seeing an unfamlilar face at the door, most people race through their mental rolodex and attempt to evaluate the potential danger. Am I in trouble? Who is this person? What do they want? Have I won a clearinghouse sweepstakes of some kind? As soon as they open their mouth your fears are realized. They're trying to sell something and take your money! Again, blood pressure elevates, pulse quickens, adrenaline flows, neck hairs raise, and the fight or flee instinct takes over. But there's nowhere to run and you're forced to fight.

Suddenly, it's face-to-face, mano a mano, kill or be killed. Your wily advisory throws the first punch, a blinding smile, which connects squarely to your jaw, followed by a flurry of probing oral jabs to the brain. You reel, dazed and confused, but regain your balance and quickly counter with a combination of wild excuses. Like a seasoned professional, the salesperson ducks, bobs, weaves, and sidesteps your best punches and throws a nasty uppercut to your wallet. You block it with great satisfaction, but they counter with a crushing overhand right to your spouse's unprotected heartstrings, followed by a blinding left hook to your ego. It connects and you crumple to the living room carpet. You're down for the ten count. Escorted by your spouse, the victorious gladiator slips through the door, steps over your body, and glides to the kitchen table to conduct business.

The Fly: "Stay out of sight. Maybe he'll think we're not home."

"Low blow!" you scream. "No fair using my spouse against me!" Moments later, while still clearing the cobwebs from your head, you write out a check for an overpriced set of cookware or a worthless insurance policy—one that you don't want—or need! You've been KO'd by the fly.

Solutions

The first line of defense in repelling flies is the door itself. If you're not prepared to go toe-to-toe with a persuasive salesperson, NEVER let them get a foot in the door! They can't sell you anything from the sidewalk, but once they pass under the lintel, they've invaded your space and have the psychological advantage. You then begin to treat them like a guest in your home, not an intruder. Two ways of deterring the fly before it gets to the door are to post a "No

Soliciting" or "Beware of Vicious Dog" sign in plain view. This strategy might not deflect every fly but it will catch a few.

Unfortunately, a good salesperson is rarely thwarted by signs. Rather, they view signs as personal invitations to supper. Others are more cunning and utilize a bag of dirty tricks to get their foot in the door.

According to Tim, an insurance salesman from central Illinois:

"Whenever I come to a house with signs posted I always stop. Those people are very easy to sell. A sign just tells me that they can't say no to anything and that they don't have enough courage to look me in the eye and slam the door in my face. If every house had a no soliciting sign posted at the door I'd be rich!"

A secret weapon that pests use is "leads."

"When I worked sales I used to purchase leads from a lead company," explained Jennifer. "Leads were the keys that opened many doors for me. In most cases they broke down all resistance. A lead is an official looking card or document which contains the name and address of the prospect printed on it, along with some general information. The information is vague, but leads the prospect to believe that I was sent by the government to present information only. Wrong! Eight out of ten people I called on fell for it and let me in. Before they knew it I was giving them a subtle sales pitch and they were giving me their social security number and signing over a check. Don't fall for some phony piece of paper with your name on it. It's just a way of getting in the door. If you do let them in, ask for the telephone number of the 'institution' which produced the information. The salesperson won't be around long after that."

In the event that an ingenious pest actually penetrates your perimeter and infiltrates his/her way into the house, it's important to establish a second line of defense. Pull back, dig in, and make your stand in the living room or in the hall. NEVER let them get to the kitchen or to the table where you normally write checks and pay bills.

*"Most families conduct business at the kitchen table,"
added Mick, a sales trainer from Missouri. "The key to
making a sale once you're inside the house is getting the
prospect to sit down with you at the kitchen table. Once
that happens, most people will even offer a cup of coffee. It's almost impossible to get a check sitting on a
sofa or standing in a hallway. If you want to keep a salesman from making a sale, don't let him in the door. If you
do, don't let him sit down at the table. That's half the
battle."*

Dale, a salesman from Mississippi, recalls a humorous inci-
dent which illustrates the strategic importance of reaching the kitchen table.

*"I once called on an elderly couple who had a large
dog," he exclaimed. "I knocked on the door and the lady
yelled 'come in!' I thought I had a live one. I stepped in
and immediately headed for the kitchen table, but the
lady insisted that I sit in a certain deep, plush easy chair
in the living room. As soon as my butt hit the chair I
sank several inches into the cushion. Suddenly, a fero-
cious-looking 100-pound pit bull came bounding in from
the kitchen and hurled itself on my lap. He totally sur-
prised me and I couldn't move. We were damn near nose-
to-nose and he looked real mad. Apparently, I was sitting in his favorite chair. I thought I was a goner. Instead of biting me, he gave me one long lick from my
chin to my forehead. Then he collapsed on my lap and
began whining and wanting me to scratch his belly. The*

old couple couldn't stop laughing. This had obviously happened to other salesmen. I tried to get the dog off my lap but he wouldn't budge. I spent an hour talking to those people about their dog and I never got the chance to sell them a thing. Worse yet, the dog was shedding terribly, and I left the house with dog hair all over my new suit! That was the only time a dog ever kept me from making a sale!"

If after an exhaustive battle you're still losing ground to a pugnacious salesperson, it's time for a last ditch effort. But the situation is grim. The fly has you pinned down at the kitchen table under heavy fire. Casualties are mounting. Willpower is knocked out. Morale is low. Money is in grave danger of being captured, and the cavalry is nowhere in sight. What can you do? The answer is best revealed in a battlefield message sent from the French general Foch to his commanding officer during World War I, "My left is rolled up, my right has been driven back, and my center has been crushed. I shall attack!"

But with what? Ingenuity and malice, what else! If you can't beat 'em join 'em. If you can't resist saying yes, simply say yes— but agree to pay only by check. Then stop payment on it after the fly buzzes happily out of your house. This may cost you a stop-payment fee at your bank, but it will dislodge the person from your kitchen table and force them to repay their company for any advance or commission they receive for the sale. If this strategy isn't to your liking, tell the salesperson that you agree to purchase their product tomorrow at such and such a time after your unemployment check arrives. Or, tell them to come back on the weekend (their day off) and then conveniently be away from home. They'll get the hint, especially if you leave a note stating that you've changed your mind and decided to take an extended trip. Be sure to apologize for any inconvenience you might have caused and provide them with the phone numbers of several neighbors whom you dislike. It won't be long before the pest either pulls out of your neighborhood or sells your enemies a shiny new set of cheap pots and pans.

Conclusion

One person's pet is another person's pest. For some, religious solicitors. telemarketers, salesmen, beggers, lawyers, bums, and even the homeless qualify as pests. For others, pests are family, friends, co-workers, or anyone who causes a minor inconvenience. But one thing is certain, everyone has them and everyone has their own definition of what a pest is. Therefore, it is impossible to lump them all into a single category and attempt to perscribe a panacea for ridding the world of them. But it is safe to say that pests will always exist. Co-existence is simply a matter of deciding what you can live with and what you choose to live with. Now that you have the awareness and the skills, the choices are yours.

TO DO LIST

1. Never buy a product or service over the telephone, no matter how good it sounds.
2. Request the full name, name of the supervisor, and phone number of the solicitor or salesperson.
3. Post a "No Soliciting" sign by your door.
4. Get a dog—**a big one!**
5. Look ahead when walking or jogging. Avoid beggers. But in isolated places carry a pocket full of small change for beggers. Don't take a chance on getting hurt over a little money.

7

CONCLUSION

This book has focused on the relationship between a small number of selected parasites and their hosts— the dynamic between the users and the used. It is by no means a comprehensive work. Examples of parasitic behavior are as vast as human experience, and it would be impossible to identify each one. Instead, this book has taken a broad tongue-in-cheek, yet very realistic look, at an age-old condition—that of how to identify and rid our lives of some of the people who use us.

The reality is that everyone uses everyone to a degree, and as long as we occupy Village Earth we will continue to do so. We are social animals by nature and are dependent upon one other. We cannot, nor were we intended to live our lives without human interaction. It is what sustains us and disappoints us, angers us and inspires us. But life is too short to waste on those who do not enrich, improve, or add to our lives in some measure, however great or small. Therefore, ridding our lives of parasitic people, not all people, should be our aim. We should strive to avoid contact with those who detract from our well-being and maximize interaction with those who enhance our lives.

"There must be some place else that's open."

Ultimately, our aim should be to learn more about ourselves, because in the final analysis, most of what happens to us is because of us. We are largely responsible for our own lives, our own fortunes, and our own misfortunes. Therefore, we must better manage time, resources, and relationships. Instead of blaming others for our fate, we should seize control of our own lives, relinquish control of others' lives, and **refuse to be used**.

THE LUP TEST

Since you have read this far, it is likely that you see yourself as a frequent host to an array of Losers, Users, and Parasites. But, it is also likely that you have witnessed some of your own LUPish behavior, either past or present, within these pages. Therefore, all that remains is for you to take the LUP TEST to determine if you too, are a LUP. As with the HOST TEST, answer each question truthfully.

1. Do you cry on friends' shoulders more than they cry on yours?
2. Do you often borrow small personal items, such as jewelry, stamps, stationary, tools, etc., from people and fail to return them?
3. Do you make it a habit to visit people during meal time?
4. When invited to dinner do you never take a gift of wine, candy, flowers, or anything else?
5. Do you believe that the world is your oyster?
6. Do you contact friends and family only when you need something?
7. Do you borrow money and conveniently forget to repay it?
8. Do you spend more than one night a week at someone else's house?
9. Do you borrow a car more than once a week, or do you often ask others for a ride?
10. When you are a passenger in someone else's car, do you "forget" to offer to pay for the gas?
11. Do you make long-distance calls from someone else's phone and "forget" to offer to pay for them?
12. Do you accept gifts and favors and never return the kindness?
13. If you smoke or consume alcohol, do you do so only when others have it?

14. If single, would you marry a person whom you didn't love, for money?

15. If married, would you divorce and re-marry some one else for money?

16. Do two or more articles of someone else's clothing hang in your closet?

17. Do you sample/taste food from other peoples' plates without their permission?

18. Do you believe that it is better to receive than give?

19. Do you arrive at potluck dinners with no pot (we're not talking "grass!")?

20. Did you borrow this book?

Total up the number of questions that you answered "Yes" to, and consult the following table to learn your LUP Level.

LUP Test Scoring Table

0	Certified Host
1 - 5	Exhibits mild LUP tendencies, but there is hope.
6 - 10	Mid-level LUP
11 - 15	Certified LUP
16 - 20	Buzz off and buy a book!

Losers, Users & Parasites

ORDER FORM

Pathfinder Publishing of California
458 Dorothy Ave.
Ventura, CA 93003-1723
Telephone (805) 642-9278   FAX (805) 650-3656

Please send me the following books from Pathfinder Publishing:

_____Copies of **Beyond Sympathy** @ $11.95 $_____
_____Copies of **I Can't Do What?** @ $14.95 $_____
_____Copies of **Injury** @ $9.95 $_____
_____Copies of **Living Creatively**
                   With Chronic Illness @ $11.95 $_____
_____Copies of **Losers, Users & Parasites** @ $9.95 $_____
_____Copies of **Managing Your Health Care** @ $9.95 $_____
_____Copies of **No Time For Goodbyes** @ $11.95 $_____
_____Copies of **Quest For Respect** @ $9.95 $_____
_____Copies of **Sexual Challenges** @ $11.95 $_____
_____Copies of **Surviving an Auto Accident** @ $9.95 $_____
_____Copies of **Violence in our Schools, Hospitals and**
                   Public Places   @ $22.95 Hard Cover $_____
_____   @ $14.95 Soft Cover $_____
_____Copies of **Violence in the Workplace** @ $22.95 Hard $_____
                   Violence in the Workplace @ $14.95 Soft $_____
_____Copies of **When There Are No Words** @ $9.95 $_____
                                              Sub-Total $_____
                   Californians: Please add 7.25% tax. $_____
                   Shipping* $_____
                                              Grand Total $_____

I understand that I may return the book for a full refund if not satisfied.
Name:_____

Address:_____
_____ZIP:_____
Credit Card_____ Card No. _____
*SHIPPING CHARGES U.S.
Books: Enclose $3.25 for the first book and .50c for each additional
book. UPS: Truck; $4.50 for first item, .50c for each additional. UPS
2nd Day Air: $10.75 for first item, $1.00 for each additional item.
Master and Visa Credit Cards orders are acceptable.

Losers, Users & Parasites